One-Sentence Approach to Story Crafting...
learning to say more with less

Kelly Swanson

One-Sentence Approach to Story Crafting…learning to say more with less

Introduction

Dear Reader,

I would like to think that you already have an interest in crafting a story or else you wouldn't be here. Or perhaps you are here by force and would rather have your left arm sawed off than share in my overwhelming passion for putting words together. Or maybe you're somewhere in the middle - somewhere in between admiring my font and appreciating the fact that you could be having a root canal instead. Take comfort, oh ye of little faith, for I am convinced that in the pages of this manual you will find something that will make writing more fun or at least less painful.

Whether we hear it in the classroom, the office, the stage, the church pew, or the telephone, we all love a good story. Stories entertain us. Stories connect us. Stories teach us, empower us, encourage us, and convince us. Stories cross barriers. Stories have amazing power. They can also put us to sleep. Picture yourself at a party where mingling is necessary. Now picture that guy who's wobbling slightly and telling everybody within earshot the fascinating story of his trip to Myrtle Beach for the yearly CCITH convention (Concerned Citizens for the Improper Treatment of Hamsters) – a story that starts three years before with a thirty-minute preface about how he came to be involved with such a passionate group. And by the time he's finished, your eyeballs are rolling back in your head and you've seriously considered faking a heart attack if he goes on any longer. Know what I mean? How about that financial speaker who loses you in the first thirty seconds by telling you about the priest, the rabbi, and the lawyer who walk into a bar? Or the motivational speaker who speaks in a soft quiet voice that drones on for so long you actually consider killing yourself. Do I lie?

I have heard so many poorly crafted stories that didn't have to be. Stories that with the use of a few tips and techniques would have been one hundred percent better. Stories that had great potential but never got off the ground. I found myself saying, "If only they would move that around and take that out, the story would be so much better. If only they knew that the first paragraph was unnecessary. If only they knew that they should have made the character do this instead of that. If only they knew that story could have been told in five minutes." We're not talking rocket science here. We're talking about some simple basic techniques to help you write a better story. If you're interested read on. If not, well then maybe you can line your bird cage with this manual.

Thank you for taking the time to hear what I have to say. I hope that by sharing what I have learned I will ignite a spark in you.

All my best,

Kelly Swanson

Kelly totally changed the way I write my stories. What used to be a daunting task, is now fun. She has made writing easy for me. She helped me lift the burden of feeling like I had to tell my audience everything. She showed me how much better it is when you use fewer words. She didn't just help me fix a story. She changed the way I approach every story. I can't wait to get home and rewrite them all. If it worked for me, it can work for you. Janet Harllee – storyteller, writer

About Kelly...

Kelly Swanson is a nationally known award-winning author, comedienne, and storyteller. She tells funny stories about life in the south using her wacky cast of southern characters who live in a place where tater guns misfire, beauty pageants abound, and fine art comes on black velvet. Her one-woman shows have delighted audiences from coast to coast. She has performed at the National Storytelling Festival, the *Best of Our State* Festival, opened for Loretta Lynn, has appeared in numerous conventions,  festivals, schools, churches, businesses, social events, and is a repeat performer for Holland America Cruise Lines.

Her work can be found in print (*Aunt Vyrnetta...and other stories from Cedar Grove*) and various CD's, one of which has won awards from the National Parenting Publications Association and the Film Advisory Board for quality family entertainment. Whether you see Kelly from the stage, the podium, or attend one of her *Comedy*, *What's YOUR Story* or *One-Sentence Workshops*, you are always in for a side-splitting good time. Not only are Kelly's shows high-energy, entertaining, motivating, and informative, she weaves into her comedy poignant messages that encourage, inspire, and remind us to stay on the funny side of life.

Kelly currently serves as 2006-2007 President of the North Carolina Storytelling Guild, as well as past Secretary and Regional Representative. She is a member of the National Speakers Association and an active member in its local chapter, NSA/Carolinas. She can be reached at: Kelly@kellyswanson.net, or www.kellyswanson.net, or 1-336-889-9479. She offers private coaching upon request.

What this workbook is NOT...

This manual is not for you seasoned writers who already know these basic tips - unless you didn't learn them the first time around. This manual is not the place to find stories for your repertoire. If you're still struggling to figure out what stories to tell, then you need to back up and read my *What's YOUR Story* manual which is geared at helping uncover the story inside of you. And this manual is most certainly not intended to force you into a writing process that you don't like. It is merely a suggestion and what works for me. Take it as you will. Use all or none of it. I don't care. That's the beauty in being a writer. You control the words you use.

The value of a story...

I challenge you to find a job or a role in life that doesn't benefit from the use of a story. Parents use stories to teach their children. Managers use stories to connect with their employees. Companies use stories to sell their product. Counselors use stories to help others through difficult times. Teachers use stories to prove a point. Pastors, speakers, performers, musicians....I could go on and on. Stories have tremendous power to encourage, inspire, motivate, and persuade. Stories cross culture, gender, and age barriers. When you have a point to make, it's not the information that people buy into - it's YOU. And the best way you have to show them who you are, is through a story. If you still need more convincing, read Annette Simmons' book, *The Story Factor*. Stories are a valuable tool. But it is even more important that the story be told **well**. A poorly told story can be worse than no story at all.

Table of Contents

A LITTLE ABOUT ME...

Hello. My name is Kelly Swanson and it's nice to meet you. No, you haven't heard of me. Most people introduce me as "up and coming" which I've learned is a polite way of saying *this is the best we could get for fifty bucks*. I recently opened up for Loretta Lynn and was so honored to have been asked. But I told them that it was like asking Booker Diggs to open up for Hank Williams. You're probably thinking *who the heck is Booker Diggs*? That's exactly my point.

In case you can't tell by my accent, I'm from the South. I'm from a place where we keep our sofas on the front porch, our refrigerators in the garage, and our cars up on blocks. We think fine art is a set of those plastic geese scattered in the front yard, that road kill is just fast food, and the closest thing to heaven on earth has got to be NASCAR. We spend Saturday mornings roaming flea markets trying to find another set of ceramic pig salt and pepper shakers, or maybe a unicorn airbrushed on black velvet.

I'm a performer, which means I love the stage, I love the lights, and I'm about one bounced check away from living in my car. When you're a storyteller like me, you often get paid in chicken. Try depositing that down the plastic ATM tube over at the bank. And storytellers don't get asked to be on the cool shows like Leno or Oprah Winfrey. We get asked to be on the local cable channel's featured artist of Buncam County, in between Tyrise and Sharonda's back yard wedding, and that one-armed pastor who heals people. But it's good exposure. And there's chicken.

I met a professional speaker who convinced me that there is a place for me in the world of professional speaking. Me and my funny little stories about life in the south. Go figure. A corporate speaker? What did I know about professional speaking in corporate America? Shoot, I thought meeting planners were those nice leather bound calendar things on that rack in the back of Staples.

I thought back-of-the-room sales were the clearance tables in back of the Wal-Mart where haggard women scrapped over that last purple thong at half off.

I had product, I just never considered selling it. I went to perform on my first cruise ship and didn't even take my books and CD's because I needed the extra suitcase for my shoes! What did I know about clients and brochures? Shoot, I thought a testimonial was something Baptists did after they got religion.

I didn't consider myself smart enough for Corporate America - like my husband who lays awake at night pondering the mysteries of the universe. I lay awake at night wondering what happens to their tattoos when big people lose weight. Or how do veterinarians get their dogs to pee in a cup?

I thought a speaker's bureau was something filled with sweaters that you stubbed your toe on in the middle of the night and how cool that those manufacturers named furniture after speakers. Kind of like a parson's table. I thought finding your niche was something you didn't talk about in public. And to me, gross profit was a pretty accurate description of my income.

So don't come to me for advice about marketing. I don't know all there is to know about the speaking profession - or even close. But the one thing I do know is how to tell a good story. And how to help you do it too. Whether we're speakers, preachers, performers, teachers, parents - there's a story in all of us. Hopefully, I can help you find it. Or even better, help you tell it.

WHAT YOUR STORY SAYS ABOUT YOU...

The paragraphs you just read were taken from my show and speech openings. I would like for you to stop and (assuming you've never met me) think about what conclusions you have already made about me based on what you read. Based on the stories I just told you about myself - what emotions you felt. Did you laugh? Did you relax? Maybe you thought that this manual might not be as boring as you expected. Maybe you decided you are better off having a root canal. Maybe you're reaching into your wallet to send me money for a class on punctuation. No matter what you have decided up to this point, you have developed some sort of opinion about me, whether it is trust, hate, annoyance, or undying devotion. And you developed this opinion based on what I just said. Based on the stories I just told. That, my friends, is the value that stories have in your presentations. They make you human to your listener.

Whatever you speak about, I challenge you to find someone else who doesn't speak on the same thing. I don't care how much of a niche you think you've got, eventually someone's going to come along and do the same thing. You can probably find hundreds. Content is content is content. You're giving that content away every time you stand up at the podium. I'm not saying that content is not valuable. I'm saying that content is not what is going to make you stand out. It's not what will make you different. It's not what will make them choose you over the other five speakers they are considering who speak on the same subject that you do. What makes you different is YOU. It's your own personal flavor that you add to your speeches. The human element - the passion and credibility to convince your audience. Your story.

I don't necessarily mean the story of your life. Or even the story of how you came to be here today. I'm referring to your life experiences - why you do what you do - why you're up there on that platform - why you are telling that particular message. Kind of like when you're sitting at a bar and a stranger asks, "So, what's your story?" They're not necessarily asking for a detailed biography from the second of your conception. They want your story (at least that's what they claim) - the kind of story that can be told in a sentence or two. For example, if someone came up to me in a bar and asked my story, I'd probably say that I'm just a small town southern girl trying to make a living doing what I love to do.

Take a moment and ask yourself, "What's my story?" Let's go one better. Why don't you write it down?

_____

_____

_____

_____

_____

_____

_____

_____

If you had trouble writing your story in the space given above, then this is definitely the manual for you!

Stories have tremendous impact as tools of persuasion and influence. It's not your information but your story that the person buys into. It's not your product they are buying, it's YOU they are buying. They must first trust you before they will accept your words as truth. If you're still not convinced of the power in a story, then I suggest you read Annette Simmons' book *The Story Factor* that talks about storytelling in Corporate America. Or get one of my *What's YOUR story* manuals. But today we're going to assume you already have your story or at least an idea for a story. Today is about crafting that story in the best way for use on the platform.

As you go through this manual and learn my approach to story crafting, you will be crafting a story of your own. The idea for the story will come from you, so stop for a moment and think about what story you want to work on today. All we're looking for right now is the *idea* for a story. You may want to tell a story about your grandfather's first job. You may want to tell a story about the day your child was born. You may want to tell a story about a fellow you served with in the military who changed your life. I can't give you the idea. If I did, it wouldn't be your story. So think of a snapshot in the scrapbook of your life that you'd like to turn into a story. And don't pick something complicated. Start with a simple short story.

Write your idea here:

_____

_____

_____

_____

_____

If you've run out of space then you're over-thinking this. We're just looking for an idea at this point.

YOUR FIRST PRIORITY IS TO ENTERTAIN...

I don't care if you are a motivational speaker, a high-content speaker, a preacher, a humorist, a teacher, or whatever your platform - your first objective must be to entertain your audience. You may be turning up your nose and saying with a curled lip, "I am not an entertainer, I am a teacher. My words stand alone."

Well, I've got news for you and your ruffled feathers. If you don't engage your listener (and that's what entertaining is) they aren't going to hang on long enough to hear what you have to say. You must get their attention and keep it. You must put them in a place where they are receptive to your message. That is your biggest responsibility. Please do not assume that when you speak people are automatically hypnotized by your voice and can find no better joy in this world than listening to you pontificate all day - or even for thirty minutes. Even the best speakers in the world know when to quit.

With the world of technology exploding all around us, it's getting harder and harder to engage our listeners as their attention spans get shorter and shorter, and their expectations get higher and higher, and the bar continues to rise. Not to mention all the other speakers out there who have the same message you do and are working diligently to stand out above the rest. When I listen to a speaker, I usually tune in for about two minutes. If they lose me in that first two minutes, chances are good they won't get me back. Take your position on that platform seriously. Entertain your audience and they'll hang on every word you say.

Now let's take a minute and think about what it means to entertain an audience. And the best way that we can do this is to think about what entertains us. Think of your favorite TV show. What do you like about it? What about your favorite comedian? Your favorite speaker? Your favorite movie or author? What are the characteristics that keep your attention?

_____

_____

_____

_____

_____

_____

_____

Or even better, think of the worst speaker you've ever seen. The worst sermon you ever heard. That horrible show you saw on TV that you knew wouldn't last a season. That comedian that made you wish you had a tomato. What made them horrible?

_____

_____

_____

_____

You can hear a speaker talk for forty-five minutes and it can feel like a lifetime. You can hear a speaker talk for an hour and it feels like five minutes. It's all about entertaining your audience. Do that, and they will be putty in your hands. Let's move on to crafting that entertaining story.

HOW IT ALL STARTED...

The one-sentence approach has been brewing in my mind for years as I've watched countless speakers, storytellers, and performers, and realized that many were making the same common mistake. They were using too many unnecessary words. Remember that guy at the cocktail party I mentioned earlier?

It seems that somewhere along the way some of us have taken on the assumption that longer means better. Or we just like to hear ourselves talk. My mother, bless her heart, starts every story she tells with what she had for breakfast that morning. My Aunt Marge talks so much that at times she actually interrupts herself. I have a friend who will leave a ten-minute message on my machine - the first five minutes she spends talking to me, the last five minutes she spends talking to herself.

If you remember only one thing today, remember this: LONGER DOES NOT EQUAL BETTER.

THE BURDEN OF A STORY GONE TOO LONG...

Let me share with you an analogy given to me by a friend of mine (Bil Lepp, the infamous West Virginia Liar) who told me to compare my listener to a hiker. While I am speaking, that hiker is climbing a mountain carrying a backpack. And he's taking every detail I give him and loading it in his backpack. And by details, I mean characters that you introduce, events that take place, settings that you describe, etc. And that backpack is getting heavier and heavier and heavier. Don't let him get to the top of the hill and realize that he carried much of that weight for nothing. Don't give him details he didn't need. If you have a character in the story that has nothing to do with the plot, take him out. *But he's funny,* you may say. Then try to make one of the main characters funny instead. Or leave him in there for the purpose of creating humor - that is a good reason to include him. Otherwise, cut him.

(PS Since writing this manual I have visited with Bil Lepp and found that he was not actually the creator of that little analogy – that he got it from someone else who said they didn't create it either – and that it was a car, but he changed it to a hitchhiker. So mud on my face and kudos to the person who really thought of it who I'm sure would say they took it from somebody else. So if you are going to share it, I recommend that you change it from hiker to something else – perhaps a plane? Just a suggestion.)

Watch television shows. They are a good example of what I am talking about. They must be tight because they only have thirty minutes or one hour to get their story told. They have no choice but to focus on what is absolutely necessary. If you watch enough mysteries and detective shows, you will quickly learn that every character is introduced for a reason, even if the reason is to throw you off the scent in order to surprise you later.

Have you ever heard someone tell a joke and think to yourself that half of what they said was unnecessary to the joke and that it took ten minutes to get to a punch line that wasn't even funny? It's draining. If it had been short it may have been funny. But it went on for too long and the listener got tired of carrying that backpack. And the payoff was not worth it. One great rule of comedy is the weaker the punch line, the shorter the joke should be. For every second you stretch that joke out, you'd better hope the punch line is funny enough to carry the load. When in doubt, make it shorter.

Here's an example of what I'm talking about. It's a joke that I use in my shows. I'm showing you how it started, and then how it ended up. Look at sentence one (written the original way) and sentence two (written a better way) and note the difference.

1.   People call me different things - storyteller, speaker, entertainer. But no matter what, I'm a performer. Being a performer means a lot of things. It means that often you get asked to perform for no money. Especially if you're a storyteller. Most of the time we get paid in food. We don't make as much other performers do - especially the famous ones. So we aren't doing it for the money. We're doing it because we love the stage and the lights, and the people. It isn't glamorous by any means.

2.   I'm a performer which means I love the stage, I love the lights, and I'm about one bounced check away from living out of my car.

Do you see how it's possible to say the same thing with fewer words? It just takes a little practice. So let's practice on our own. I'm going to give you a paragraph and I want you to make it shorter and better by using less words, and better words. Don't stress, there is no right answer. The only correct answer will be the shorter answer.

- *Once upon a time and long ago in a place far away, there was a beautiful meadow. Oh, it was so beautiful. It was covered from one end to the other with flowers of every color. And when you walked through it, the smell just overpowered you. And you could see forever. Flowers everywhere. It was so pretty. And in the middle of this field there was this house - an old rundown house with broken shutters. The paint was peeling off and there were more weeds in the garden than there were plants. It was an ugly brown house. And in this house there lived a little old woman who had lived there her whole life. She had grown up in that meadow. And now she was old. And she lived there all alone.*

Now rewrite the sentence trying to say more with less. Again, there is no right or wrong answer. I challenge you to try and write this paragraph in one sentence.

_____

_____

_____

_____

_____

_____

_____

_____

Here's one way to do it:

- *Tucked in the middle of a perfumed meadow, stood a tiny cottage as ugly as the meadow was beautiful.*

Or another way:

- *Who knew that nestled in a meadow of such splendor lived a gnarled old woman blind to its beauty.*

Or how about this:

- *Her hands were gnarled and bent, much like the weeds which had overgrown her little cottage. They say the surrounding meadow had whispered to many a painter, just as her tiny cottage had whispered to those few brave enough to knock.*

Now let's try it with another paragraph: (You don't have to make this one sentence)

- *My mother grew up in a small town in Georgia. It was the same town her mother had grown up in. My mother was one of three children - two boys and a girl. She was the youngest. My mother, now she was an interesting woman. She was about twenty when I was born. She met my dad at the bowling alley where she worked nights. She was about five feet tall and a bundle of energy. She had once been a track star in school. Everything she did, she did fast. Without thinking usually. My mother was always doing something with the right hand and something else with the left hand. Painting the house, cleaning the gutters. She could do lots of things at one time. Like put on lipstick and drive. She did that all the time. It was tiring just watching her go. She would talk on the phone, and cook, and clean the house. She made best spaghetti in the world. Everybody talked about how good it was. My mother was nice, but she was kind of crazy. She did stuff without thinking first. And she could never make up her mind. First she'd want red, then blue, or maybe purple. One day she'd want this, one day she'd want that. It took her forever to get ready when Daddy took her dancing. The red dress, or the black? The pearls or the silver? Nothing was good enough. Had to be better. You should have seen her at the holidays. And she loved people. Loved taking people things for their birthdays - baking casseroles when people were sick. And people loved her. Even my friends. My friends all thought she was a fun mom. Not me. I thought my mother was crazy and embarrassing. She got on my nerves.*

Okay, now you try:

_____

_____

_____

_____

_____

_____

_____

_____

Here's how I did it:

- *Mamma ran on one speed, and that was high. That woman sandblasted her way through life - eyes closed, changing course sporadically, and wondering at every turn should she have gone in the other direction. One arm cleaning, another arm baking, an ear to the phone, an eye out the window, and looking for miracles every step of the way. Folks called her a passionate woman. I called her a leech on my soul.*

It's not about finding a way to include every detail. All those details are simply not necessary to the story and make that back pack heavier. It's about finding one or two details to give you insight into that character or that scene. You don't need a personal history on that character. In most cases, just a line or two will do. And that's the main theme of my one-sentence approach to story crafting - learning how to say more with less.

Many of us approach writing from the wrong direction. It's not your fault. It's the way you were taught in school. I can still hear the teacher say, "Get out a piece of paper, here's your topic, now write a three-page story. Go." We pull out a piece of paper, have a general idea of a story, and stare at the paper until we come up with a place to start and then we just go. And we write, and erase, and write again, and end the story when we're out of paper. That's how I did it for years. But that's the hard way. It's like handing somebody some wood and a handful of nails and saying *build me a doghouse - you've got twenty minutes*. No wonder so many people hate writing. It's near impossible when you go at it like that. Constructing a story would be so much easier if we put a little thought into it first. If we just did a little planning ahead.

So stop for a moment and make me a little promise. Repeat after me: I will never again begin the creation of a story by pulling out a blank page of paper, beginning with *once upon a time*, and writing until I've filled the pages up with words. I will plan my story first.

You may be saying, *Yuck, I hate planning*. Get over it. Good stories take work. Trust me, this little bit of planning will make the job of writing a story so much easier. You will spend less time this way than trying it the other way. In fact, sometimes once my planning is done, the story pretty much writes itself - especially when alcohol is involved. Just kidding.

Before you even think about writing that first sentence, think about the story for a little while. Chew on it a bit, as I like to say. If you just do this, I promise you a better story. Think about the story while you are doing other things, like driving or grocery shopping. Why are you telling it? What does it mean to you? What do you like about it? What is the moral of the story? What are the good parts? What value does it have for someone else? Is it a funny story, a sad story, both? Can you fit its message to your speech topic? What kind of audience would it best suit? What are the characters like? What's the best way to tell the story? Every character in that story is going to see it from a different perspective, so which character do you choose? How do you want your audience to feel when hearing the story? Do you want to make them laugh? Make them cry? Make them think? Surprise them, scare them? Don't get burdened down in figuring out a plot or how you will connect it all together. Just think about the big picture and the scraps that will make up your story.

Remember that idea you had for a story a while ago? Write down some thoughts about it. Not complete sentences or ideas - just thoughts.

_____

_____

_____

_____

_____

_____

_____

_____

_____

_____

_____

_____

_____

_____

Note about personal stories...

Let me take a moment to address the personal story. If yours is a personal story (as most are) then you must be able to step away from it and judge its ability to entertain. It's hard for us to be objective about our own personal stories because much of what makes them so interesting, or so funny, is due in part to the fact that they happened to us. I fall into this trap quite often.

For example, we have a funny family story about the time my mother ran into the trashcans at the mall. We can't tell that story without falling out of our chairs and peeing on the good furniture. And every time we tell it, we laugh harder than the time before. I have yet to tell that story to anyone outside our family and get so much as a chuckle. And, trust me, I've tried. And whenever I tell that story I turn into that guy at the cocktail party. It's quite humbling.

And I've often wondered to myself why that story is so funny to us and not to anyone else? Maybe you just have to know my mother, and if I explained her better then it would be funnier. (Which I tried by the way, and it didn't work.) Maybe if I told them how loud those trashcans were. (Nope…didn't work either.) Maybe if I embellish it a little and talk about what she did after that. (Nope.) Maybe if I start with what she had for breakfast.

I finally realized that this may be one of those mysteries I will never fully understand, like suck-me-in panties that take off an entire size without putting it anywhere. But when I stepped away from the story and tried to picture someone else telling me a story about their mother running into some trashcans at a mall - well, it wasn't funny to me either. My advice here is to step away and try to be objective. Picture someone else telling you that same story. If that's too hard, find someone who you trust will give you an honest opinion. Someone outside your own family. Duh.

Back to chewing on the story...

When I have an idea for a story, I walk around with it in my head for days - just thinking about it. Thinking of what I like about it, don't like about it. Sometimes my stories start with a funny image - a cherry blossom special wig shooting through the wooden blades of a ceiling fan at Erma Dean Jean Jones's bridal shower. Or a poignant image - my Granny Bee and James Perdue slow dancing in the Waffle House. Or I'll walk around with a theme in my head - a mother forgiving her son - the beauty in women encouraging each other - the power we have to make a difference right where we are. Then I'll think about what kind of story would best portray that theme.

I look around me wherever I go and watch people to see the funny things they do, the kind things they do, to hear their stories, to watch their expressions. They all get catalogued in my journal for future use. I look for something to spark an emotion. Or I'll look at my own life - what it was like growing up, trying to be popular, having a dream. I bring up images from my past - my first grade teacher, that scary room in the basement of my house, the plastic pink hairbrush.

One day, as I mentally explored my childhood, I came up with some material about growing up in my house and getting in trouble. It turned into this:

I have a two-year-old at home which still qualifies me as a new parent. I'm what the pregnancy books call a "seasoned" mother which means I've gone from "Oh, look, a brand new mommy" to "Good grief, are they still getting knocked up at your age?" Now that I'm a parent, it astounds me how much has changed since I was a kid. Kids today have got it made.

Today they actually have Mommy and me classes! When I was growing up we watched soap operas through the playpen bars and that thick smog of menthol Pall Malls, while our mammas played bridge and complained about house work. Kids today have Wriggles concerts and Disney on ice. When I was growing up we sat around in hot living rooms staring at each other and watching Uncle Edsel pop out his teeth in between verses of "Keep on the sunny side."

When kids get in trouble today they get time out. When I was growing up, we got spanked. Hard. In the front yard. By somebody else's mamma. It was an unspoken rule that a mamma could spank any kid on her property that was misbehaving. That's why none of us played at Jimmy Van Cuso's house. Shoot, his mamma could draw blood, and not even spill her drink.

Depending on who you asked, tools of torture varied, from the switch, to the belt, to a pair of faded flip flops. In our house, they were more culinary in nature. Like the wooden spoon, the spatula, the waffle iron. And on occasion, the plastic pink hairbrush. My mamma could do some damage with hair products. And being as I had what today they'd call ADD, back then they just called you the demon seed, I was on familiar terms with that hairbrush. I walked around for the majority of my youth with the term Goody tattooed on my rear end.

Mamma would spank you silly with that thing till it broke. And then you'd get blamed for it. "Now look what you made me do." And any other spanking-related injury she'd incur, like stubbing her toe or dislocating her shoulder. The plastic pink hairbrush. It's no wonder I can't walk down the hair aisle at Walgreens without suffering a flashback.

We used to get paddled in school by the principal, Mr. Butkus. And we'd be sitting there in music composition singing "Mine eyes hath seen the glory," knowing full well that Jimmy Van Cuso had been caught in the girls' locker room again and a paddling was near at hand.

The thing about those paddlings, was that you could hear them all over the school…the rhythmic whack of the wooden paddle up against that denim-clad rear end. And that sound would travel - down hallways, across lockers. Shoot it would go three stories up and into that open window where we sat singing, "Mine eyes hath seen the glory….WHAM. Of the coming of the Lord…. WHAM. No law and order detectives coming to save you. No social services. Honey, you were on your own.

Why to this very day, I can't hear that song, without clinching my butt cheeks in honor of Jimmy Van Cuso. Excerpts from *Now Look What You Made Me Do...* by Kelly Swanson

There are stories all around you. Just look for them. And you don't have to look for a whole story - look for just a snapshot - an image - something that triggers an emotion.

When I was first married, my husband's father was very ill. His mother had just passed away and it was a matter of time before his father went too - probably more from a broken heart than the illness that had ravaged his body and left him stripped of everything from his pride to his memory. My husband became his constant companion - not so much the dutiful son as the son who had the joy of calling his father his best friend. And it was tough on us as newlyweds, because priorities had to be shifted to take on this task - especially with us in NC and his father in Maryland. And each evening we would talk on the phone (me in NC and my husband up there) and I'd ask how his father had been. And each evening it was usually some dismal report on his father's declining health.

But one night when I talked to my husband and said, "How's your dad?" I heard, "Well, tonight was a good night. Tonight Dad took my mom dancing." And my husband described the look on his face and the slight twitch in his feet. And that image stayed in my head for weeks until finally I had to let it out. And here is what it became:

Did you know that every Friday night, Frankie Scarpetta goes dancing? He puts on his best blue plaid suit and his yellow polka dotted tie. Slicks back his hair, splashes on some cologne, and takes his wife dancing. Oh how they dance. She still smells just like a sweet magnolia blossom. He still looks in her eyes like no other woman ever existed before her. He still sings in her ear, slightly off key as usual. And they dance. Frankie's wife passed away fifteen years ago. That dance hall is now a pump and go. The band has parted ways. Frankie never leaves his bed over at Sunnyside Hills. And most days, he doesn't even know his own kin from somebody else's. But every Saturday night, Frankie Scarpetta, goes dancing.

WRITING YOUR ONE SENTENCE...

You should now have a pretty good idea of where your story is going. If you don't, stop, and get that straight before we go any further.

Now that you're ready, it's time to write your story in one sentence. It doesn't have to be a good sentence, or include all the major points of your story. It can't be a sentence that has fifty words in it. Just write a sentence that tells someone what the story is about, including the value, the moral, or the message of the story - what it means to you. This is not an easy thing to do, so take your time. It will get easier the more you do it.

Pretend you're on an elevator and someone has asked you what your story is about. Think of it like that deep voice you hear on a movie trailer telling you what the movie is about in one sentence. *Death and destruction hit a small town where hope finds its way through the dark.* This will take some thought because we aren't looking for plot here, just an aerial view of the story and the meaning it holds. And, again, we aren't looking for entertaining words, just get that sentence out. Let me give you an example of a one-sentence description of the classic fairy tale called *Beauty and the Beast*.

- Beauty and beast come together in this touching love story about true beauty being in the eyes of the beholder.

Someone else may have a different way of saying it. That's okay. Stories mean different things to different people. The point is that I want you to know what is important about your story. And if you can't find its value, or what it means to the listener, I question whether it's the right story to tell. And sometimes (especially if you are a humorist like me) your story may not have a deeper meaning. It may just be a silly story about Aunt Vyrnetta's cherry-blossom-special wig getting caught up in the wooden blades of the ceiling fan at Erma Dean Jean Jones's bridal shower. That's okay too. There is certainly a place on the platform for stories that are intended to make people laugh. Just get your story down to one sentence.

Please note that this one sentence will not be the first line of your story and will probably never even show up in your story at all. This is just preliminary stuff to get you ready to write it. To get you focused on the heart of that story. To keep you from taking tangents to get there. To give you a starting point.

Go ahead and write your one sentence. You can practice on the back if you want.

_____

_____

_____

_____

_____

_____

_____

This may be confusing to you and you may question its relevance. But I have coached many storytellers and writers who are telling stories without any clear idea of what their story is about. Some discover that their story is not really about any-thing - just a series of events tacked together that they thought sounded interesting. If your story isn't about anything, it won't mean anything to your listener. And when you aren't really clear on what your story is about, it is harder to focus on the details that are necessary to the story. When you think about the story you are going to tell, think about what that story has taught you. Why it has stayed in your heart. Why you need to share it. Let's move on to the next step.

WHAT THE READER NEEDS TO KNOW...

Now that you have your one sentence, you need to decide what the reader NEEDS to know for the story to make sense. What are the details that are important to the story? They don't have to be interesting right now. We're just looking for a list of the important points to your story. And I highly recommend that you make an actual list.

How do you know what's important to the story? For example, it's not necessary that we know how Cinderella's father dies or where the three little bears went when they left their cabin. We don't need to know if the Grinch had brothers or sisters, or what time span was covered in the three little pigs. It's not necessary to start a story with what you had for breakfast or a three-page description of a meadow. Don't start the story about your mother with her entire lineage dating back to the Mayflower.

There are some things that we do need to know for a story to make sense. We DO need to know the main character's conflict. Why is Cinderella sad? We DO need to know what made Beauty fall in love with the Beast. We do need to know who the story is about – the main character and something about that main character's personality and appearance. We do need to know what happens – the plot. We need answers to questions like *who, what, when, where* and *why*. We need to know how conflicts are resolved. We need to know what you took away from that story. These are just ideas to get you going. Every story will have its own unique list of important details.

Now it's time to make your list. It doesn't have to be perfect. You can change it later.

_____

_____

_____

_____

_____

_____

_____

_____

_____

_____

_____

_____

_____

Now stop a minute and pat yourself on the back. Many people don't ever bother to plan out a story ahead of time. You have just saved yourself time and energy. If you don't follow any more of my advice, your stories will be better just having done these two simple steps. And if they weren't that simple, don't worry, it will get much easier the more you do it. Eventually, it will become automatic. If not, you gave it a good shot, now go hire someone to write your story for you.

PUTTING THE NECESSARY DETAILS TOGETHER...

You should have a list of details that are essential to the telling of your story. It's time to put them together. We are still not worried about making it sound good at this point. Just get it down on paper in the order that you want to tell these details. For example, if you were telling the story of Cinderella you would probably start with her living situation, then her problem, then how the problem gets fixed, etc. This is the part where we are actually organizing the plot – what goes first, what happens next, etc. Sometimes I will stay in a list or outline format for this part and just move around items on my list until they are in the order that they need to occur in the story.

Go ahead and put together your necessary details below:

_____

_____

_____

_____

_____

_____

_____

_____

_____

_____

_____

_____

_____

Good job! The hardest part of the writing process is over. And I guarantee that it was easier this way than starting with a blank piece of a paper and "Once upon a time…" Now you have the basic structure of your story. It is probably quite bland at this point. That's okay. You have a good solid foundation. Making it interesting will be the easy part. So let's get to it.

TIME TO ADD THE FLAVOR...

By flavor, I'm referring to the spices that will make the story better – that will change it from boring to interesting. Why add flavor? Because a story that just relays a series of events is not interesting. I've heard so many people tell stories about their relatives that were just long historical accounts, as if the teller were leaving it up to us to find what is interesting in the story. Well, I'm sorry, but you don't get to put that burden on your listener. Trust me when I say that they won't go to the trouble. You have to make your story interesting to them. You have to force them to participate. You must pull them in. That's entertainment. So how do we make a story entertaining?

- By keeping it short and saying only what is necessary
- By giving it rhythms (fast paced, slow paced, high voice, low voice, silly then serious, etc.)
- By mixing thought, dialogue, and action
- By surprising your audience – go against what they think you will say
- By reminding them of their own lives
- By finding universal themes that all audiences relate to
- By making the listener look at things from a different perspective
- By making your audience laugh
- By painting a picture for your reader where they can see, hear, smell, taste, and feel
- By letting them know what that story means to you and why you tell it
- By writing as if we are talking to our listener, not at them

Those are just a handful of ways to make stories more entertaining. There are many more. But you've already got enough suggestions to make your story sing. Now you get to add the spices to your own story. Remember that we don't want any spices that don't enhance the taste. Make sure you have a reason for putting them in. Ask yourself if it is really necessary to the story. Does the audience need to know that to make it a good story?

Here are some easy ways to add flavor to your story:

- Describe your main character (remember you only need a detail or two)
- Describe other necessary characters (even less information than the main character)
- Add a little dialogue (just a phrase or two is all you need)
- Describe your setting
- Put some humor into your story
- Put some emotion into your story
- Create exciting openings and closings

Start writing some things that immediately come to mind when you think about adding flavor to your story. You will work on this again later in much more detail after we discuss more ways to spice up our stories. But go ahead and write down the spices that are immediately coming to mind. You can always cut, so write as much as you want.

How long should stories be?

You may be wondering how long your story should be, especially after reading the heading above. Should it be a page or ten pages? Should it be one minute or twenty? Let me begin by saying your story should be as long as needed to tell all the necessary information. Some stories need to be longer because there is more to say. Longer stories can be written in pieces as if you are constructing a series of short stories and connecting them together.

Never write a story to fit a certain amount of time. Write a story to fit the story. Worry about the time later. Keep in mind that you can always edit your story to fit your time later. I would recommend that you keep all your stories for your speeches to five minutes or less to fit the short attention span of today's standard audience. If you follow my One-Sentence approach, you are forced to write the story in one sentence and then build on that. That's the difference in this method of writing. You are starting with one sentence and adding on - piece by piece.

Let's talk some more about this one-sentence approach using a story from my portfolio. The idea for this story began when a woman told me she had a nude portrait of herself painted for her husband for his birthday. The woman was not a small woman, and the image of her portrait hanging over their bed stuck in my mind. I kept thinking that there had to be a story in there somewhere. And something told me it was going to be funny.

So I got out a piece of paper and started to write. Three pages later, it wasn't going anywhere, it wasn't as funny as I had intended, and I couldn't figure out where to go with it or how to end it. It wasn't interesting. It wasn't funny. It wasn't about anything really except a lady getting painted on black velvet. The problem? I didn't plan it first. I had skipped the most important part. So later, when I came up with this new one-sentence approach, I dusted the idea off and starting chewing on it. What did the story mean to me? Why was I telling it? What would be funny about the story?

I started to play the *what if* game that I often play when thinking about stories. What if I made this a story about *my* mother? Aha, it just got a little more interesting. And what if it was a painting done on black velvet? Now we're getting somewhere. And why not talk about other things my mother did to embarrass me. Now surely people can relate to that.

And what was my story about? Was it about more than a series of events leading up to a painting? Of course. It was a story of how my mother taught me to live every moment - even if it means painting yourself on black velvet. And that became my one sentence. Easy as that.

Then I had to ask myself what else the reader needed to know. I came up with this list:

- Mamma's quirky traits - a brief description of her personality

- How she embarrassed us to no end - my teenage view of my mamma

- Why she got herself painted on black velvet

- What that looked like

- How we felt upon hearing the news of her plan

- The unveiling of the portrait and the family's reaction

- How he day ended

- What I learned from the whole thing

See, it's not an extensive list. Just the main points. Then it was time for me to add flavor to the story. Let's talk a little bit more about adding flavor.

More about adding the flavor...

At this point in your story, you are ready to find some interesting details to add – some spice. Now you want to try to find more interesting words to use than the ones you've chosen - descriptions that are unique. Find a way to replace three sentences with one. Here is where you want to enhance the emotions – insert the jokes – add your own personality to the story. The key is to keep it tight and remember that your goal is to say more with less.

I have often found that a story can be improved tremendously with just the slightest flavor added to it. With each spice you add, it gets better and better. Sometimes something as simple as a funny sounding nickname is all it takes.

It is my own personal belief that there are always ways to improve a story – ways to change the spices, ways to add more flavor. Where to stop is up to you. Just know that giving your story that extra attention will make all the difference.

STOCKING YOUR SPICE RACK...

When it comes to adding flavor to your story, there are some spices you should always have on hand. These are some common tips and techniques for crafting a short story.

OPEN WITH A BANG

The opening of your story is one of the most important lines because its purpose is to get the attention of the reader and keep it. If you lose their attention in the first minute, chances are good you won't get it back. Use this opening wisely. Many people will take this chance to give background information leading up to the event, or to describe a setting at great length. Or they will spend ten minutes telling you about the story they are going to tell you. I think this is a mistake. Nothing makes me angrier than someone who talks for fifteen minutes and then starts their story. At this point I don't want to listen to them, I want to hit them.

Start paying attention to the first chapters of books you are reading, or to the beginnings of movies. There are many creative ways to start a story. You can start with your own thoughts. You can start at the end and then back up. You can start with the most action-packed scene in your story. Use the opening to GRAB the reader and let them know that this is going to be good. Foreshadowing is a great technique to use in the beginning and will be discussed in a moment. But first I want to show you some good openings and bad openings.

- Once upon a time...   BAD
- Now I'm going to tell you a story about my mother....   BAD (just start
  the story)

- It was my mother who taught me that sometimes our greatest weakness can turn out to be our greatest strength…..
  GOOD
- Who know that cold morning in December would change my life..   GOOD
- Granny Bee had always dreamed of living the fancy life…   GOOD
- There was once this enchanted forest filled with all sorts of exotic plants and flowers. They were so pretty and it smelled so good. And the sun came shining through the trees on the tiny drops of water on the petals. And the forest was so thick you couldn't see further than two feet in front of you. And you could hear all the animals chirping and singing, and the frogs croaking. And on mornings after a heavy rain, the wet leaves would stick to your feet…..

                                    BAD (Who cares?)

Compare opening sentence 1 with sentence 2:

1. Once upon a time there was a pond with floating green lily pads. And in that pond their lived a family of frogs – mamma frog, daddy frog, sister frog, and brother frog. There were also many more frogs that filled up that pond. There was one frog who was king of all the other frogs and his name was George. George was a very proud king and considered himself to know more than anyone else on the pond.
2. George was king of the pond and proud of it.

Sentence two jumps right into the story. You have time to let your listener know he's a frog. But see how much more interesting sentence 2 is when you just jump into the story?

Compare opening sentence 1 and 2:

1. Once upon a time, long ago and far away, there was a kingdom. And in this kingdom there lived a wicked queen and her daughter named Snow White.
2. She had one more opportunity to kill the beautiful princess. She needed a plan and it needed to be good.

Isn't number two much more exciting?

FORESHADOWING

To foreshadow is to hint that something will happen later. It fills your reader's backpack with anticipation – and therefore keeps their attention. Foreshadowing is very effective in the beginning of your story, but can also be used in other parts of the story too. Just remember not to give away the surprise. This is only supposed to be a hint.

Example: The heavy wind howled throwing tree branches against the side of the house, as if it knew what danger lie waiting within.

HUMOR

I could spend an entire manual on humor alone. In fact, I do have a comedy manual. It's a broad subject – one that's worth exploring if you have the time because funny always sells. But if you want some quick ways to make your story funny, try these:

- Give your characters quirky nicknames.
- Give your characters flaws – we love it when people aren't perfect – make them clumsy.
- Use accents and voices.
- Insert your own funny thoughts into your story. You're allowed. You are the narrator.
- Surprise the audience. Humor is often found in places where you set the reader up to expect one thing and then give them another.
- Find ways to incorporate a joke or two into your story – takes a little work to make it flow, but it can be done.

The best advice I can give you about making your stories funny, is to start keeping a journal of funny things. Start looking in life for those funny moments. Write them down. You don't have to turn them into stories, just capture the funny. Then when you are writing your stories, these funny things can be worked into your story. The journal was the best thing I ever did for my comedy writing. The more you look for the humor in life, the more you start finding it.

LIE

Your goal is to entertain, not to stick to the truth. There are times when lying in your story is not ethical. I don't think you should lie about having cancer, or having a degree in psychology. There are other things you probably shouldn't lie about either. I'll leave that up to you. But when it comes to the tiny details of a story, don't sacrifice your story just to keep it truthful. You are a writer. That means you have the liberty of making anything you want happen in that story. Try to step away and see the story as fiction and what it needs to make it more interesting. Look at it like you are exaggerating the story. That's the hard thing about personal stories. The truth is often not interesting enough. If you have a problem changing it, then find another story to use.

CHARACTERS / DETAILS...

Here are some helpful hints I've picked up along the way that you can think about when creating characters and other details in your story:

- It's not the plot that makes the story, it's the people. I believe this to my very core. My stories are about people. Life is about people. Your audience relates to the people.

- Allow your characters to be themselves. Give them subtle differences in speech. Note that all of your characters won't react to a situation in the same way. And remember to be consistent once you have established certain traits in your character.

- Don't play the joke – play the character.

- Make characters real enough to be believable – the reader will only suspend disbelief so far.

- Give your characters complexity – like a child with an imaginary friend who is a British soldier with a hat so tall it won't fit in the back seat.

- Find ways to breathe life into your characters.

- Use your similes and metaphors.

- Remember your five senses. Describe how things smell, look, feel, sound, etc.

- Know your characters. Stay away from "flat" characters. Understand them, write bios about them. You don't have to write all of that information in your story (please don't) but know them that well. Especially for serious longer pieces with a strong main character. Remember that it doesn't take a lot of words to bring your character to life. Sometimes you will find that a description can be a sort of story in itself. I often use character sketches for little fillers in my programs. Think about how your character reacts to things, as humans react to things. Put yourself in the situation of the main character like an actor would for a movie. Basically, we are striving to make our characters real.

- Look for weird personality traits in people, dumb things people fight about, stupid things that break up families. Look all around you – real life has all the material you will ever need.

- Always try to SHOW the character's reaction instead of telling them. Let the action carry the day. Sometimes one sentence of dialogue from that character will tell you more than three paragraphs of description.

- Create families and characters that everyone can universally relate to – especially when using humor. Phone books are a great place to find the perfect name for your characters.

- Remember with dialogue that less is more. We don't need to hear everyday conversation.

- You have a lot of power in your incidental characters – those characters that float around the story. Make them realistic and interesting. They can provide humor when your main character can't.

THE DESCRIPTION GAME

Here's a little game to play to get you used to describing things in unique ways.

Describe the following items **WITHOUT** using the words written below the item.

1. Sun

    a. Hot

    b. Round

    c. Yellow

2. Orange (the fruit)

    a. Juicy

    b. Orange

    c. Round

3. Standing on a sidewalk in the middle of August

    a. Really hot

    b. Sweating

4. Holding a newborn baby

    a. Tiny

    b. Smells good

      c.   Little cry

   5. Loss of a loved one

         a.   Sad

         b.   Cried

   6. An ugly dog

         a.   So Ugly

   7. An old tennis shoe

         a.   Stinks

         b.   dirty

Show don't tell – with descriptions and actions

Whenever possible, show me, don't tell me. This takes works, but gets easier the more you do it. Don't tell me she was crazy, show me how crazy.

> *Crazy Katie lived in a world other people didn't. She saw things other people couldn't see. Heard things other people couldn't hear.*

Don't just tell me John Henry was a troublemaker, show me.

He didn't just get into trouble, he looked for it. And more times than not his trouble all started with five little words. Five innocent sounding words that never failed to lead John Henry Junior down the road to ruin. Wouldn't it be funny if… Wouldn't it be funny if he put soap bubbles in the fountain out front of town hall? Wouldn't it be funny if he put super glue in old Widow Jenkins' bicycle seat? Wouldn't it be funny if he dropped his pants and mooned the marching band?

Don't tell me your cousin was tall and skinny, show me.

Horace was so skinny when he turned sideways he up an disappeared, with feet so long the from the side he looked like a capital L, and a long neck with an adam's apple that bobbed up and down like the lure on a fishing line.

Don't just tell me she was a large woman, show me.

Aunt Bitsy was not a delicate woman, by anybody's definition. Her rear end was so large that there were days when it actually looked like her hips were in parenthesis.

Don't just tell me he was mean, show me.

Alabaster Cripe was a nasty man - mean beyond belief.

He never laughed and he never smiled, why we weren't sure he had teeth.

Alabaster Cripe was about this tall with a head as bald as a tater,

A chin like a witch and an eye that twitched and a mood worse than a gator!

At this point, you may have some inspirations of your own. Want to take a minute and come up with some descriptions of your own?

_____

_____

_____

_____

_____

_____

_____

_____

_____

_____

_____

_____

_____

_____

_____

Same goes for action - show instead of tell. Don't tell me she ran fast, show me.

She ran faster than a plump turkey the day before thanksgiving.

When she ran it took her rear end an extra day just to catch up.

Aunt Bitsy started clogging and, bless her heart, there were parts of that woman exposed that only the good Lord Himself knew about. And every one of them was shim-

mering and shaking wildly back and forth to the beating rhythm of them marching pumps, like some kind of country choir where everybody's a struggling to be the solo.

Same also goes for feelings - show instead of tell. Don't just tell me she was sad, tell me *that the lines of her face were pulled downward – like the strings on a puppet.*

And often times you don't need to even describe the emotion. There are times when the action can take care of that too.

He still looked in her eyes like no other woman ever existed before her.

CLOSINGS...

The common mistake many storytellers make comes in not knowing when to quit. When you have resolved your conflict and ended your story, end it. Short and sweet. Sum it up with a quick little note about what you learned, or something that ties it all up. But don't keep talking. Don't explain what the listener should have learned from the story. And then explain it again. That's called spoon feeding your reader. Readers like to come to their own conclusions. You don't want them to sit there thinking, "Okay, I get it already!" Sometimes you can just end the story without having anything to say about it. And it is always better to quit while you're ahead. Quit while they are still enjoying the story. Just one page more can hurt your story.

CUT, CUT, CUT, WALK AWAY, AND THEN CUT SOME MORE...

When you are through with your story take a break. Get away from it for a while. Then come back and see what you can cut. Cut and cut wherever you can. Then walk away again. Come back in a couple of days. And cut some more. The tighter you get your story, the better it will get. I promise. Then you can have someone else read it and give you feedback.

THE BIG PICTURE....

I don't see big stories anymore. I see snapshots. I see moments. Scraps. And I work with each scrap until that small piece is finished. Then when I do a show, I start putting scraps together. And you don't need a lot of words to connect these scraps. Sometimes you don't need words at all. These scraps can turn into bigger stories or just sit there in a portfolio of stories that you have for your presentations. Stories that can fit different audiences. A portfolio that you will continue to update with new scraps. It's that easy. And it all starts with one sentence.

RECAP...

Okay, you've learned a lot today. Let's review:

1. Think about your story first – what it's about, what it means, why you tell it
2. Write your story in one sentence
3. List what the reader needs to know
4. Add the spice
5. Cut until you can't cut anymore

Okay....are you ready to try it on your own? Now it's time to write your story.

_____

_____

_____

_____

_____

_____

_____

_____

_____

_____

_____

_____

In case you still don't get it...

In case you're still having trouble understanding how this works, I will show you the process with another story I wrote. It's a story that only takes me six minutes to tell.

The idea started when I met a bluegrass band who told me that when their gig got snowed out the night before, they ended up having a late night meal over at the

Waffle House where they brought their instruments inside and ended up giving a show - a free show - right there in the Waffle House. For some reason that image stuck with me. I could just see the people in that Waffle House, seeking shelter in the storm and drawn together by music.

I had to think about why it stuck with me. What did that story mean to me? Why had it affected me? I decided that it meant something to me because it was the story of something neat happening in an unexpected place. I didn't want to tell their story because I had convinced them to turn it into a blue grass song of their own. And it was their story. But I still liked the idea of neat things happening at the Waffle House - the idea of beauty in life occurring in unusual places. How could I capture that same idea? And the story began to emerge as a snapshot of an old couple slow dancing in the Waffle House.

So I had this image in my head of an old couple dancing in a Waffle House. And I walked around with this image for days, still not sure what the story would be about. Finally I decided to fall upon a common theme for my writing - the road more traveled – people with unrealized dreams. And I saw a message of hope - that life is what you make it - and sometimes we get something even better. Yeah, that's what my story was going to be about. It was time to write my one sentence.

This is the story of how my Granny Bee's unrealized dream taught me that sometimes life gives you something even better than what you ask for.

That was my one sentence. Not a fancy sentence. Not even well written. But it really captured the essence of what this story is about and helped me to focus on what needs to be said to get that point across.

Then I listed the necessary details:

- Granny Bee has a dream
- What is the dream
  - she wants to dance
- What makes her want to dance?
  - Seeing her first movie
- She doesn't get the dream - why? (Want real life issues that people can relate to)
  - Mamma sick - doesn't have time for lessons
  - Daddy loses his job
  - She ends up working at the bakery all day
  - no time for silliness
- But she still dreams
  - even when she marries
  - even when she had children
- And then the dream fades - at least the hope of it coming true
- And I am sad that she never got her dream - and I want the audience to be sad too
- I see her and Grandpa dancing in the waffle house
- And she is happy - as if all her dreams have come true
  - And you can tell she has no regrets
- And how I feel that sometimes we don't get our dreams - we get something even better

These were the points that would make up my story and its plot. Then I looked for ways to add flavor:

- I wanted a sense of long ago
- I wanted the scene in the Waffle House to be pivotal
- I wanted there to be a connection between her dream and her reality

Now the story was ready to write. And to my surprise, it was really already put together with not much needed to wrap it up. Here is what it turned into:

Granny Bee had always dreamed of living the fancy life. Ever since she saw her first picture show, and that beautiful movie star gliding across that stage in the arms of that handsome man with a suit that had tails hanging off of the edges. And he was singing in her ear.

And that day, in that very moment, a dream was born in Granny Bee. A dream of dancing her way to stardom. And she was going to have silky blond hair, whisper-thin high heels, and dresses that billowed around her ankles like she was skating through the clouds.

And that dream lived in her just about her whole life. But sometimes life's callings don't match our own. And Granny never got to finish those dance lessons 'cause Mamma took sick and she had to help take care of the younguns after school. And she couldn't buy those fashion magazines once Daddy lost his job over at the paper mill. They didn't have money for such luxuries.

And she never got those whisper-thin high heels. It didn't make sense, her being on her feet all day over at the bakery. But she still dreamed. One day she'd have that fancy life. And when she met James Perdue and fell in love, she warned him that one day she'd have that fancy life so he'd better see fit to travel.

She married Grandpa Jimmy on a Saturday morning, in front of a Justice of the Peace. She was wearing a pale blue suit and a matching hat. It took every last dime they had to buy their first house - you know the one - the one with the green shutters over on Front Street. She still talked about the fancy life, just when the children grew up. And then the children grew up and had children of their own, and she didn't talk about it so much. But every once in a while you'd walk past her knitting basket and see once of those fashion magazines lying on top.

I was driving through town one evening (about fully grown by then) and I passed by the Waffle House - the one they're trying to tear   down over on Main. And I saw Grandpa Jimmy's truck out front. I thought it was awful late for them to be out, so I pulled in to see if I could be of any assistance. I never even got out of my car. I just sat there in that parking lot, staring through that dusty diner window at the sight of my Granny Bee and James Perdue, slow dancing in the Waffle House - eyes closed, hands clasped, barely moving. Probably to some old forgotten tune on that rickety jukebox. Granny had this dreamy smile on her face like she was a million miles away, wearing *whisper thin high heels and dresses that billowed around her ankles like she was skating through the clouds. And Grandpa Jimmy was singing in her ear.*

They buried Granny Bee in a simple pine box with a simple marker. They didn't see fit to put more than her name and the dates. But in my mind, her tomb stone will always read, "Here lies my Granny Bee, who dreamed of the fancy life, and got something so much better." Granny Bee, by Kelly Swanson

So in closing, writing shouldn't be seen as this unconquerable beast. When you take it apart or rather put it together, bit by bit, it's quite easy. Look at it as if you're putting together scraps. Just remember to say what only needs to be said. Less is better. That's key. Write your story in one sentence. Then add the necessary details. Then swap out the boring way of saying it for better ways to say it. And cut, cut, cut, cut. And if you are still having trouble, take my extended One-Sentence Workshop or Coaching Sessions. We'll find the story in you.

PERFORMANCE TIPS / HELP WITH YOUR DELIVERY...

Often I will hear stories that are crafted in a manner that does do justice to the story but is not delivered appropriately. Delivery is just as important as having a good story. Lack of either can cause you to lose your listener in just a few moments.

One of the most important factors in your delivery is your comfort level on stage. I don't care if you have pee running down your leg and you're fighting back the urge to vomit. I don't care if your leg is shaking or a sweat has broken out on your forehead. DON'T LET IT SHOW. The best way to not let it show is to SMILE. Smile and act like you're having a ball. When you are visibly uncomfortable so is your audience. When you have a painful experience and your audience sees it, then they have a painful experience. You're audience becomes embarrassed for you. So practice looking comfortable. You can also practice for things that may mess you up on stage – like forgetting lines, a roaring train in the distance, etc.

Your voice is a powerful tool allowing you to hit different ranges from high to low, to take on different character's voices, to elicit emotions, use accents, to change the tone of your story. Play around with your voice when working on a story. Sing, chuckle, hiss cluck your tongue, hum.

I like to look as storytelling as a dance between you and your listener. Our eyes are the connection. They demand the attention of your listener, for one. They bring the listener in, like you are engaging them in a conversation. Get comfortable looking at your audience. The eyes can be used to express emotions like fear, surprise, anger, etc.

Use your facial features as a means of taking on the persona of different characters by a slight change in facial expression.

Timing is very important in a story and not something I can really teach you how to do. It is something that takes great practice. Timing is not only important in humor but also is important in piecing together your story. Stories follow a certain flow that could be the focus of its own workshop. Stories usually start low, build up to a point, and then drop back down. Some follow different patterns, like a joke's abrupt ending, etc. Sometimes the flow of a story can be messed up by waiting too long to introduce the conflict, by ending before you've really resolved everything. The best way to work on your timing is to practice for a friend who is familiar with writing/storytelling, and can listen to your story for timing tips. I can help you if you need it.

One piece of advice I can give you that really falls into several different categories, is giving people a change of pace. It's a trick I use to keep the reader engaged. It's combining funny and sad, high pitch with low pitch, grand gestures with small (unless your style is like Donald Davis, which works well too). Basically, it's giving the audience breathers, a change of pace, commercials in a sense. You are constantly refreshing your performance so that they don't get too used to seeing the exact same thing. What you don't want to see (the far extreme example) is a sort of monotone performance, with no movement, no gestures, your voice in the same pitch, etc. Shake things up. I want to start doing this in my stories as well. Break up a heavy sad scene with humor or a poem. Sing a verse. Go off into a monologue. Know when you've kept them down too long and need to bring them back up.

One thing I try to remember when crafting my stories is to keep them conversational. What I mean by that is that you are not speaking <u>at</u> your audience you are speaking <u>with</u> your audience. I think the biggest difference in my delivery happened when I stopped getting up on stage and reciting a story and started sharing my stories instead, savoring their details, enjoying them right along with my audience. Even though they don't speak back (usually) you are both communicating with each other in a different way than an actor or an actress. Have you noticed how off balance you feel when on a stage with a bright light in your eyes? You have to act like you are looking into their eyes. Remember this as you write/edit your story. There is a difference in the story meant to be read and the story meant to be told.

PUTTING IT ALL TOGETHER (PLANNING A SHOW)...

Often as tellers we freak out when we faced with our first opportunity to do a concert type of performance or when we have an hour to perform and we want to do several stories and tie them in together somehow. This proved to be easier than I thought it would be when I stopped trying to come up with a theme and then stories to match. Instead, I chose the stories I liked and worked on how to link them together or to find/create a common thread to connect them.

First, determine the value you want to bring them. That's the first thing I think about when I'm contacted by a potential client. If it's a storytelling festival, ask yourself who is in your audience. If it's an annual corporate meeting, what are they there for? If it's a celebration, what are they celebrating? What message do you want to take to that audience?

I also found that marketing a show adds a little extra spark above simply marketing yourself. I found people showing more interest in my program called *Mamma and the prom, and other reasons I need therapy* than they were in just hiring me, Kelly the Story-teller. And I didn't write a new program I just took one of my stories that had a catchy title (very important here) and used that as my title. When I titled my program, I had no idea what stories I would do. I titled another program called, *Pieces of*

Heaven and other spiritual truths from Cedar Grove. That left me open to do Pieces of Heaven and any other stories I wanted to do. So I would suggest coming up with a catchy title to describe one of your stories and create a theme around that. Then pick stories that fit that theme.

There are many ways to connect them together. You can connect them by using your own thoughts in between as connectors. I use my "not much going on in Cedar Grove" to connect my stories. Find something in one story that can "remind" you on stage, of something from another story. Let's try to do some of this together and see if I can show you what I mean.

Once you've learned to do this, you can start selling shows. I'd suggest having a portfolio of stories ranging from thirty seconds, to a couple of minutes, to twenty minutes. Fill your program with different sized pieces.

WRITING EXERCISES...

Try some of these fun exercises. You will find that many will trigger ideas for stories. Because I'm in the business of making people laugh, you will notice that many of these techniques involve humor. But I still think they're good and you should use them whether you're funny or not.

1. Find new ways to describe objects – come up with an object and rule out what the person can not use to describe it, leaving them with no choice but to come up with different ways to describe something. For example, describe the word "sun" without using yellow, hot, or round.
2. Write a very ordinary situation involving ordinary people. Then rewrite it introducing a conflict that affects the group, making sure you exaggerate the events. Choose one of the characters as the narrator making sure they see the funny side of the picture.
3. Make a list where your character encounters situations that defy the normal ideas of logic and reason, where innocence is defeated by ignorance and communication is defined by narrow parameters. And then give your character different reactions to each situation. For example:
   a. Recorded messages at large companies that lead you to other messages
   b. Employee doublespeak
   c. A rigid company policy
4. In this exercise there is no interaction with your character and anyone else. Your character's inner thoughts describe a situation where life's dirty tricks either run rampant or amble gently. Your character can also make comment on another character's behavior. For example:
   a. Your character sitting in a restaurant commenting on the other diners
   b. Christmas dinner with the relatives
   c. The work place
5. Take a dramatic situation from the past and retell it in a humorous way
6. Find annoying situations in life that are universal and write about them (ex. At the gym, automated customer service, traffic, grocery store lines, etc.)
7. Take an ordinary situation and ask, "What if this happened?" Then ask again and create another scenario.
8. Get magazines and start looking through the ads for potential humor.
9. Write a scene where a character has had "one too many"
10. Part A:Write a 2-page character outline of a regular person. Then try to put that person in a situation where things go terribly wrong so the reader, not the character, thinks it's funny.
11. Part B: Take the same character and this time make him/her humorous. In other words create someone about whom if we met in real life we would say "what a character"
12. Make a list of character traits that best describe a humorous character
13. Create a scene where 2 characters begin a conversation and a 3rd character oblivious to their situation intervenes in a humorous way

14. Create a scene where your character or characters are faced with an external event that has humorous connotations (a stuck-somewhere situation)
15. Create a scene where one character with serious intent is thwarted by an incidental humorous character

HUMOR...

I'd like to include some material in this manual on humor because I think you should use it if at all possible. You don't have to be a standup comedian but funny sells. Humor makes a speech better. Some of the most prominent storytellers in the industry are those that use humor on a regular basis. I am not the expert on what is funny. But funny is what I do. And I would like to share some things that I have learned that make being funny a whole lot easier if it doesn't come naturally to you – and even if it does.

First of all, understand that for every 10 attempts I make at writing jokes, I end up keeping one or maybe two. It takes a lot of free writing to come up with the good stuff. I will often work on something then walk away from it and come back weeks later and read it. Then I really know what's funny and what isn't. Sometimes I will scrap the whole thing altogether.

Try to be universal in your humor – this means humor that people can relate to. Not everyone (or even most people) in your audience will have seen that episode of *I Love*

Lucy when she locked herself out of the car. So don't use a line from the episode and expect people to laugh. If you are a paleontologist (whatever that is) unless you are at a paleontologist convention, don't make jokes that only a paleontologist will get. To some of you this may be a no-brainer. But really examine your humor. What works for a group of senior citizens is not going to be the same thing that will work for a college fraternity. Some examples of universal humor are those things that we can all relate to on some level whether we have directly experienced them or not. Things like dating (male vs. female in relationships), trying to lose weight, aggravation of automated customer service, bad airplane food, etc. We don't have to have ridden in an airplane to get the joke. The trick is to make sure that your audience has the same points of reference as you.

TEN STEPS TO A FUNNIER YOU ... COMEDY TIPS FOR BEGINNERS

Humor is one of the most valuable tools you can have in business. Not just in business, but in life. Not only does it entertain your listener, it makes you human. It makes you likeable. And if people like you they will listen to what you have to say. People love to laugh, and no matter what your topic, you will be at an advantage if you have a reputation for being funny. Not everybody can be a comedian. That's the bad news. And for some, there is no hope of ever being a comedian. That's worse news. But there is a place for you somewhere in the middle. That's the good news. There are ways to put humor into presentations no matter who you are. And that's why I'm here today. To give you ten steps to a funnier you.

1) Funny isn't always in the form of a joke. Find a funny story to tell that someone else wrote. You may be silly, act out wacky characters, use puppets, accents and voices. Find jokes on the internet and slip then into your routine. Have some funny comments you can make to people in the audience and use them over and over. What matters is that your humor fits your personality.

2) Find ways to incorporate humor into your story. It doesn't have to be a funny story filled with jokes, or a story that ends in a punch line. Disney movies are a great example of how humor can be woven into a story. Here are some ways to add humor:

a) Give your characters unusual names - a silly name goes a long way

b) Give your places unusual names

c) Give your characters real personalities - flaws and all (we love characters that can't seem to get it right.) It is okay if the character doesn't always make the right choice. It's okay if they mess up - and sometimes even funny.

d) Take an actual joke and turn it into a story. But I caution you to KEEP IT SHORT. The weaker the punch line, the shorter the story leading up to it. And if you're not sure how strong the joke is, make it short. If the joke is strong, make it short. Get my drift?

e) Surprise your audience. Go against what they think you are going to say. Build up suspense and lead them in a certain direction, only to surprise them and turn a different way

   i) Example: Tater had the most enviable gift in Cedar Grove. A gift every kid wanted for miles around, clear over to Buncam where his legendary name was whispered in awe. And, oh, what a gift it was. Not the gift of being able to sing like a bird, run like a gazelle, or paint like DaVinci. No, Tater had the one and only gift of its kind. (Pause) Tater could barf at a moment's notice.

   ii) Notice in the example above that I gave the character a funny name. I named a funny place (Buncam) and I built suspense. I made you think he was going to have a serious gift. And then I paused and hit you with the surprise.

3) Use the comedy rule of threes. Funny things happen in threes. I can't explain it, but it works. Here is an example: I'm a performer, which means I love the lights, I love the stage, and I'm one bounced check away from living out of my car.

4) Practice your timing. So much of comedy is timing - or the proper use of your pauses. Here are some timing tips:

a) Talk slow. They are hearing your words for the first time. Let the words sink in.
b) Pause before you make a joke. But not too much. This will take practice.

c) Pause after you make a joke as if you are merely taking a breath. Some comedians will actually take a sip of water, adjust their shirt, or freeze their face in a silly position.

d) Never start talking again until they are finished laughing. If you do, it's called "stepping on your laugh." You don't have to wait until the very last person stops laughing (that's too long) - just long enough for your audience to enjoy the moment.

5) Watch other comedians, study them, and take note of what makes them funny to you. You will probably find that it is a combination of:

a) Material
b) Timing
c) Facial expressions
d) Persona (their personality on stage)
e) Props

6) Fake it. If it doesn't get a laugh, act like it wasn't supposed to be funny in the first place. This is very easy for storytellers to do since we don't have the pressure of creating a joke every minute.

7) Punch lines go at the end of the joke. The funniest part of what you are saying needs to be at the end. Reason? People are laughing. Whatever comes next will not be heard. You need to end that line on the joke. For example, I have a line in one of my stories where I have plucked my eyebrows completely off and I say, "It was freaky. I looked like a mannequin head, I did." After telling the joke several times, I realized that nobody every heard the little emphatic "I did" at the end of the joke because they were still laughing. Finally I followed my own advice and cut it.

8) Use your face and body gestures to enhance the laugh. Come out of your comfort zone.

9) Don't assume that if someone doesn't laugh it isn't funny. People react in different ways. Some people clutch their sides and laugh out loud. Others chuckle. Others look at you like you dropped off the moon. That's the thing about humor; it's a matter of opinion. What's funny to one will not be funny to another. But if NOBODY laughs, then it's definitely not funny. Big deal, pretend it wasn't supposed to be.

10) Was it Mark Twain who said *brevity is the soul of wit*? Whoever it was, it's true, true, true. The best advice for any storyteller, writer, comedian, speaker - anyone telling a story - is to SAY MORE WITH LESS. Spend some time cutting your piece. Then cut it again. Then walk away, come back, and cut it again. Swap out a phrase for a couple of words. Swap out three words for one better one. I can't say it enough, and if you remember only one thing today, remember that. Learn to say more with less.

BOMB IN THE POST OFFICE

by Kelly Swanson

It's hard to know where to begin the story. Do I start with the ceramic rooster paper towel holder that sang *Jingle Bell Rock* and swayed its hips? Or the singing frogs with matching crocheted Santa hats? Or the tangle of orthopedic shoes sprayed with Christmas glitter? I guess I'll start with why I was standing there that Saturday morning when the bomb exploded in the Post Office.

It was two weeks before Christmas and I'm thinking of a million things I'd rather be doing than mailing Mamma's Christmas gift to her sister Bertice – that heinous ceramic rooster that cost $2.99, took twelve batteries, and from its moment of conception faced a destiny of dusty display tables at low budget flea markets waiting for a home. I pictured the death of my social life should anybody from my college see me holding this rooster and wearing the sweatshirt that Mamma made me that had my baby picture with Santa decoupaged on the front and surrounded by silver bells.

Mamma knew the rooster was tacky. That's why she bought it. It was an innocent pawn in an unspoken ongoing feud between my Mamma and her sister Bertice over who could give the most annoying gift, though I'm not sure Beatrice was aware she was playing, but may just in fact have been merely a victim of poor taste. But it all started when Bertice bought Mamma one of those life-sized resin statues of Marilyn Monroe which was bad enough 'til Mamma found out it was a fountain of all things. Being the polite southern woman she was raised up to be, Mamma had no choice but to honor the gift by putting it in her garden where it scared every bird in Garnett County and Mamma's beloved tom cat, Buttons, who was last seen on the overpass out by Brigg's trailer. And whether Bertice meant any ill or not, Mamma had been trying to get her back ever since. That rooster was going to get her a lot of points even if it cost more to ship than she paid for it. And that's how I happened to be standing there the day the bomb went off in the Post Office.

Looking back, I can see how it was the perfect combination of things that allowed such an event to take place. One of those scenes that you could never create again if you tried. The faint ringing of the Salvation army bell outside the drugstore where Old Man Jenkins stood smoking Camels and making eyes at the girls from his shop class. The smell of Old Widow Jenkin's perfume that was part lemon, part vanilla, and part Jim Bean which folks politely refrained from commenting on. The air was crisp outside, but hot and thick inside the old post office whose walls whispered the secrets of well-meaning folks who'd taken the road more traveled. There was the lingering air of sadness for the boys whose seats were empty in church on Sunday because they were out serving their country proud according to some and serving their country in waste according to others, because even in our small town folks disagreed on the subject.

There was the fading fear of anthrax in mailboxes replaced with the fear of the bird flu that had everybody thinking twice in the produce section no matter how silly it seemed. Just the right mix of small town ingredients to allow for an event like this or even perhaps create the need for an event like this – much like the need to let the air out of a balloon that's been filled too tight.

I was seeing my home town through different one-semester-of-college-out-in-the-real-world eyes. And one semester was all it took to bring me up to speed with the rest of the world and convince me that I had in fact been living in a bubble all these years. So with a newfound passion for changing the world with my yet undiscovered talent, you can imagine my quiet desperation standing in line on that Saturday morning while Winnie Cooper argued with Hank, the Post Office clerk, over whether her card was oversized or not. Winnie was the sort of person who went beyond cheap. She bought surprise gifts to her friends with the receipt attached, as if finding the gift was gesture enough, good grief, you don't expect her to pay for it too?

I didn't hear the popping noise. I don't suppose anybody did except for Armalene who was holding the said package at the time. Realistically, the popping noise was not loud enough to create panic in and of itself, but Armalene was. She was the sort who instantly reacted to a given situation without bringing her brain along for the ride. The same sort of person with the very penchant for cutting corners and a grudge against her husband who as usual didn't put the packing tape back where he got it and in her overzealous desire to prove a point, she decided to bind his mother's Christmas gift in scotch tape, would serve them both right and maybe he would start buying gifts for his own mother after she received this two-foot-tall lamp with the colored bubbles and a handwritten note that said "for the table beside the antique Victorian settee in the living room." Who would have thought Christmas gifts could be so spiteful?

Yes, one person was all it took. One person who already had the word *bomb* on her brain because after this she was going over to Juanita's house for the going away party of her cousin Buster who had enlisted and they were gathering to have a covered dish supper and to bathe him in prayer so he wouldn't get himself blown up. And so when she heard that popping sound, well, her sense of imagination was faster than the speed of her reality and by the time it registered in her brain (though I question it having stopped there at all) the popping sound had grown in intensity and danger to the level of explosives, though she had never heard a bomb explode before and had nothing to compare it to, and without considering the logic of instilling panic in a closed-in space headed for smithereen status, she did the only level-headed thing she knew to do in a situation of this nature. And that is how one person was all it took to hear an inconsequential popping noise and scream "Bomb" at the top of her lungs, throwing the package in the air and diving under the postage counter just like she'd seen them do on that last episode of *Law and Order*, praying the whole time that when they found her poor flattened body they would not notice her grandma panties. And in the most horribly tragic moment of her life all she can picture is those back-stabbing cousins of hers crying mock tears and making sure that every one in town gets filled in on the shocking news that Armalene Dean Merriwether was not the sexy vixen she portrayed herself to be.

Armalene screams and pitches forwards and the package sails backwards and hits Cleo in the head causing her to drop her toy poodle, Daisy, who is currently napping in his seasonal holiday dog carrier with rhinestone studded letters that spell "Merry Christmas from Santa Paws." From where I'm standing I can see Cleo and Daisy fall backwards into this group of boy scouts who'd come to send their Christmas letters to the troops and are extremely excited having heard the word bomb and the potential opportunity to see their first dead bodies because being part of a bomb explosion was even more interesting than when Danny's dad caught his eyebrows on fire trying to help him get his camping badge.

And that's how Frank Junior fell into Harold, who fell into Larry, who fell into Sparky, the pudgy kid who'd had one Snickers too many, who fell backwards into me and knocked that two dollar rooster right out of my hand where it goes flying through the air and hits Sara Beadle upside the head convincing her that she's been shot and she hits the floor, landing on top of her handmade Christmas gift for her prison pen pal Slash – a drawer sachet filled with baby powder – despite the fact that according to her cousin who was quite knowledgeable on subjects of the convict persuasion, told her that prison cells don't have chester drawers – but shoot, it was just too cute for words, and she'd even hand stitched Psalm 183 on it and she wasn't taking it back now since she'd put his name on it and everything, and chances were pretty slim she'd ever come up on another Slash again in this lifetime so re-gifting was out of the question.

So she lands on top of this sachet and it busts and white powder goes floating through the air of that post office and once Terri Jo Lean catches sight of it, well it's all over after that, as she starts screaming, "Amtrax, amtrax, it's that dreaded amtrax, we are all gonna die! I keep telling ya'll we aren't safe here, after all, we are the sweet potato capital of the world!"

Well, the powder didn't sit too well with the oxygen tanks belonging to the senior citizens who were part of the *Young at Heart* Work Group brought in to help with the extra post office holiday work load and they start wheezing and coughing and losing their balance which is how one of them ended up tripping over Horace, the post office cat who belonged to the janitor who's only condition for taking the job was that he could bring his cat Horace so the kids at home wouldn't kill him.

Horace, who's front right leg was in a full cast, was not exactly in the best of spirits before this whole incident, having just been released from the vet whereupon he had his entire body shaved, not to save him from some life threatening illness but to save him from the embarrassment that follows a cat when a certain 5-year-old member of its parent family decides to play hairdresser with the family feline. And after his home perm and highlighting he was put into a dryer to fluff up and then was the unwilling participant in an experiment to prove that a cat will not land on its feet when thrown from a second story window – even if that's what happened on the cartoon channel.

So this poor cat with the shaved body and the cast on his back leg now found his tail caught under the sole of Edsel Van Meter's Naturalizer tennis shoe and poor Horace let out a wail and went sailing through the air, surprisingly fast, with the cast jutting out to the side, and he lands with a splat up against the giant poster of Uncle Sam and slid down the wall arms and legs splayed out to the side, praying that this would be the end and wishing that suicide attempt had worked a couple of months back when he'd found Jim Darling's sleeping pills only to discover they weren't sleeping pills but in fact some natural form of herbal bowel regulator which is just a whole other story in and of itself.

While the cat's sliding down the wall, and the senior citizens are tangled up in the boy scouts, Wade Jenkins acts on instinct and attacks who he is sure (thanks to his ailing eyesight) is none other than a terrorist standing in front of him that he'd had a bad feeling about the whole time and surely it was one of them Taliman's what with the dark skin and the bulky midsection, and wearing that turban looking thing and he was gonna take him out or die trying, 'cause Wade was a hero waiting to happen.

So he tackles what he believes to be the source of the bomb and finds that taking out this dangerous Taliman was easier than he expected especially upon discovering that it was a woman and no stranger at all, but rather his very own neighbor Noreen who was dressed up as a shepherd for the Cedar Grove Baptist Christmas pageant and had developed a recent addiction to the tanning bed brought on by her desire to look good in her new strapless gown she bought for that holiday cruise.

So they both fall over on top of Charlie the shopping mall Santa who had just run in on his break to get a stamp for the Christmas card he'd bought for Angelina Jolie, on account he couldn't go see her for Christmas this year, what with the restraining order and all.

Meanwhile Percy Widebottom, the newly appointed day shift manager of the post office, one of those types of employees who is obsessed with following the rules, is now standing on top of the counter screaming out the proper procedure for a fire drill – well, the manual didn't say anything about bombs – what was a manager to do? And he is screaming out "Stop, drop and roll people, stop drop and roll" and sadly enough most of the folks were doing just that, as if their very lives depended on it.

And I am standing there reflecting on that poor ceramic rooster's quick demise and the status of his eternal salvation and watching Percy Widebottom screaming at the chaotic crowd to quiet down despite the fact that they were already quiet and he was making quite the fool of himself as the sirens grew louder and police rushed in to take control of a situation with a passion that can only come from small town cops whose most exciting day until now had involved a ladder and a cat.

Surprisingly enough the whole episode only lasted for a couple of minutes. And word traveled faster than chicken pox in a day care. Folks came running towards that post office searching for possible loved ones who may have been caught in the rubble that was almost was, and before the fire chief had his hose rolled back up (don't ask) there was already a line of hot casseroles and congealed salads on the post office counter and a prayer chain that stretched two counties over. And TV shows were interrupted all afternoon as the local news picked up the story, and day time soap opera Christmas parties were all interrupted with the breaking news of a suspected bomb in the post office that turned out to be a false alarm and let that be a lesson to us all, and left folks feeling as if we had somehow dodged a bullet.

I had to break the news to Mamma that the ceramic rooster was no more and let's see the bright side in all of this as he was probably carrying a strain of the bird flu anyway and his death saved a nation. And Mamma's tears were dried two days later when she found the complete set of mooning elf dinnerware complete with mooning elf salt and pepper shakers for all for a whopping $1.99 at the truck stop on Route 9 over in Buncam.

It's a silly story that will always fall short of being deemed worthy of re-telling even though Jared who bags groceries over at Peabody's says it's a story that the tabloids would pay a lot for, that his cousin got paid $25 for his story about the aliens impregnating his chinchilla farm. If you had asked me in that moment, I would have said that story was further proof that my town was full of idiots and there was nothing to be gained from living in a place where progress and growth had stunted.

But if you had asked me later, you would have gotten an entirely different answer because it was a story whose impact came much later. After I learned that Mamma had cancer. After we had tried everything and gained nothing. After the disease had taken residence in Mamma and stripped her of most everything she held dear.

Good days were when she was comfortable. Better days were when the pain lessened. And the very best days were when Mamma laughed. And so we sat with Mamma and held her hand and wiped her brow and adjusted her pillows and told her stories. And sometimes when the pain got really bad she'd pull me close and whisper, "Remember the ceramic rooster?" And that's all she'd have to say and I'd start out with the ringing of the Salvation Army bell and the smell of Widow Jenkins perfume – part lemon, part vanilla, and part Jim Bean, though folks politely refrained from commenting on it.

the end

Closing Comments:

I'd like to close with some words of encouragement. Being an artist or a speaker or a writer takes a lot of courage. Courage to pour yourself into your art. Courage to stand on a stage and put yourself out there for all the world to see. I applaud your courage. Recognize that our gifts take work and practice and will not be perfect on the first try. Don't settle for less. Understand that for every ten attempts you may hit on one good thing. And that's okay. Never become complacent. Always push yourself to that next level, to that deeper idea, that funnier thought, or that better sentence. Never settle.

Know that the biggest stumbling block is not lack of talent but fear. Too many people give up on their dreams because they're afraid of failing. Don't give up. Trust me, there is no greater joy than doing what you are passionate about and, yes, even getting paid for it! I have heard the advice over and over and over again to those seeking success in life: find your passion and success will follow. My friends, writing is my passion. It may be yours too or your dream may hold another vision. I wish you the best blessings in life and always know that the world is a better place with the gifts that you will add to it. And remember that it's not about the destination but the journey. If I can help you on this journey, please let me know.

All my best,

Kelly Swanson

www.kellyswanson.net
kelly@kellyswanson.net
1400 Chatham Drive, High Point, NC 27265
1-800-303-1049, 336-889-9479

Note: If this manual was helpful to you, you may want to consider taking Kelly's One-Sentence Workshop which is a more intensive study of this One-Sentence Approach to story crafting, designed to help you work on your own story. This is a great workshop for groups, and can be tailored to fit your group and your particular time frame and audience type. Kelly also offers What's YOUR story workshops that are designed to help you create a portfolio of stories to fit your particular need.

35773202R00052

Made in the USA
San Bernardino, CA
04 July 2016